Killer Hacks to Move Beyond Writer's Block

Scharla Flynn

ISBN: 978-1-7389836-2-9

DISCLAIMER

This book contains strategies to help move you through common scenarios that stop you from writing. It is intended to educate, inspire and support you on your personal journey toward resolving your writer's block. Regardless of my own results and experience, I make absolutely no guarantee, expressed or implied, that by following the advice below will improve your situation as there are several factors and variables that come into play regarding your nature and that which you are dealing with.

Primarily, results will depend on you, the experience of the individual, the situations and elements that are in and beyond your control and mine.

Liability Disclaimer

I am not a psychologist or medical doctor and do not offer any professional health or medical advice. If you are suffering from any psychological or medical conditions, please seek help from a qualified health professional.

You assume all risks (if any) associated with using the advice given below with the full understanding that you, solely, are responsible for anything that may occur as a result of putting this information into action in any way, and regardless of your interpretation of the advice.

You further agree that our company cannot be held responsible in any way for the success or failure of your efforts to move past your writer's block and the effects on your business as a result of the information presented in this book. It is your responsibility to conduct your own due diligence regarding the safe and successful operation of yourself and your business if you intend to apply any of the information in any way in your life and business operations.

Terms of Use

You are given a non-transferable, "personal use" license to this book. You cannot distribute it or share it with other individuals.

Also, there are no resale rights or private label rights granted when purchasing this book. In other words, it is for your own personal use only.

CONTENTS

KILLER HACK TO MOVE BEYOND WRITER'S BLOCK

Writer's block is essentially anything that stops you from writing. It manifests in many ways and for many reasons. For one or many reasons, you struggle to move past a threshold keeping you in a holding pattern. Most of which can be determined and worked through.

The question is, are you willing to look at your writer's block honestly and work through it so that you can get back to writing or are you clinging to it because it has become a part of you—a part of how you look at yourself or what you are known for?

Here is a thorough list of things that you may identify as your block and suggestions on how to move past the block.

MANAGING YOUR TIME

Sometimes many people, not only writers, have things we want to do and things which we have to do and they conflict. You can have never-ending and haunting to-do lists, work, taking care of your family, taking care of the house and/or running errands around the city, sleep (the golden standard is still 8 hours), social commitments and events (I know I'll be hard pressed to say no to a party invite again).

Nowadays, people are much busier and our desires compete with our responsibilities. Sometimes we put the things we desire to complete on a to-do list because we intend, at some point, to do it.

If you're guilty of moving through your tasks and skipping the things (including writing if you have it on your list) that you want to do but don't need to get done for the sake of checking off some boxes, you are forsaking yourself those things you find pleasurable for a bunch of check marks. That is not an ideal strategy long term. Here's a little tip: go to the party but be wary of burning the candle at both ends.

Thankfully, you don't have to continue in this pattern. But you have to do something to make the lasting changes you desire. This is where you get to take action.

Some steps to take:

1. Brain dump. Make a list of all your current responsibilities (job, housework, your kids, etc.) and another list of all your current desires (finish your story, exercise, knit mittens, etc.).
2. Make a list of all the specific things you have to do. Be certain to put time to write on that list.
3. For one or two weeks, track everything you do and when you do it each day.
4. Being honest with yourself, look through your lists for things that no

longer serve you and also for things that you want to accomplish.

Consider if there is anything you're willing to give up or change to help you move forward with your goals. Consider focusing on writing about one idea to completion before moving on.

Once you've looked at how you spend your days, and have found the time when you can write, create a schedule that is doable for you; a schedule you can stick to and incorporate both your responsibilities and desires. Be gentle and forgiving with yourself and your time.

If you keep saying, "I have no time to write" to yourself, you'll never have time to write because what you say, you speak into existence for yourself and therefore fulfilling that very prophecy of not having time to write.

OVERACTIVE BRAIN

Your brain moves a mile a minute. You are constantly thinking about the things you have to do, or of all the what-ifs in a course of action. You keep coming up with questions about anything and everything and it impedes your writing. The rabbit holes you end up down in pursuit of the answers to these questions suck up all your time. To help yourself with this one will take some serious practice. There is no overnight fix as this is often a long existing habit. Therefore, it will take time and effort to help yourself improve your focus and calm the over activeness of your brain.

Journal. Write down everything. Empty your thoughts and questions all onto pages. Then, look at them for what they are. Question the thoughts and anything else, presenting as doubt. Are they true? Are they lies presenting themselves as truths? And are they important currently? Is there urgency with any of these? Analyze them:

- Consider what evidence you have to prove any of them as true.
- Consider if your past equals your future.
- Consider if these thoughts and questions are of your inner critic.
- Consider if they are the voices of your characters.
- Consider the importance and urgency of what you put down on paper.

Determine what is worth immediate attention or if you need to keep a blank notebook next to your writing space to empty the thoughts as they come up while you are in your designated time for writing. Doing so may allow you the time to free your brain from a rabbit hole distraction and get you back to putting words on the page.

If you find that what you're writing is actually for your story, meaning research, schedule time to conduct that research separately from your writing time, if you can.

You can also find my free 30-Day Writing Tracker and Reflection Journal on my website to help you further: www.tidepooloctopus.com

LOW TO NO MOTIVATION

You know you're supposed to be writing but you just can't bring yourself to sit down and get into your material day in, day out.

Adjust your expectations of self and know that repetitive writing is key in this case.

- Make it a point to sit down daily to write.
- Scheduling and tools like the Pomodoro Technique will help you through.
- Better yet, journal and answer the question, "why don't I have the motivation to write?"

Interestingly enough, you'll be writing. If you think it's not productive, you're wrong. It may not be progress on your project, but it is progress on yourself. This is important because by journaling why you don't have motivation will help you in future circumstances when you have the same or similar feelings.

If you currently are writing for someone else, have an actual deadline for the work (if this is for pay) and find yourself not having motivation to write, I urge you to be honest with yourself and look deep within, for why you don't have the motivation to write on the project you have been tasked with.

As you answer that question and if another question pops into your head, write that down too and answer it. Continue this exercise, answering your own prompts if they come up, in your journal for yourself so that you can see what is actually going on and what is misaligned. Once you find what that is, ask yourself how you would fix it. Ask yourself what would you like to see happen; what would you prefer to be writing about?

When you have your answers to these questions, use them to facilitate a fix in the work relationship you have. If you don't ask, the answer is always no. Ensure you do this inquiry appropriately so that if your suggestions are declined, you still have a job, your reputation is not disparaged and you can start taking actions to bring yourself to better alignment with your own being and what you would prefer writing about from now on.

Yes, you may still have to finish the project assigned to you. However, if you choose to do so, do so without throwing away your integrity. If that is compromised, think deeply on what it is you are willing to do and for what energetic exchange. Remember, you always have a choice.

WHEN YOU'RE CREATIVE BUT UNMOTIVATED TO WRITE

This can happen when your mind is everywhere else but in your writing. And you know you should be writing, but that's just not happening. Basically, your brain is in "do anything but" mode.
Create an environment and a schedule conducive to writing:

- Think of where you feel most creative and write there, if permitted.
- What is around you?
- What makes that space give you the creative feels?

- Is there a scent? A sound? A temperature?
- What do you like to see? Is there a motion?
- Are there tastes? Do you eat or drink?
- Are there people around? Are you solitary?
- Are there textures you like to feel that complete that space for you?
- Is it light filled or is there the flicker of a candle and dimmed computer screen?
- Is it tidy?
- Is it a small tight space? Is it an open space?
- Are you out in a natural setting?
- Are you writing curled up on your couch, favorite chair, desk, bed?
- Are you writing in your car, the library or a museum?

Write a list of things that inspire you. Think of the things you like or places you've been to or want to go to. Then write why you like these things and places. See? You're writing.

Alternatively, you can try the exercise from earlier and answer the question, "why am I not motivated to write?"

You could also do something else that creatively interests you. Try doing something that brings you joy or peace and also allows you to work with your hands differently, such as creating pottery or painting. If you're into hooks and needles, have at it. Crochet, knit or sew a small project.

This is to help you see the fruits of your labors as it could be that writing is a long-term game and process to which you just need to see your creativity shine through in a finished product "in the meantime" or in the short term. This can bring that sense of satisfaction you need short term. But then, get back to your writing.

Do you like to cook? Perhaps what you crave is a little time with a few friends and a good meal. Maybe the company and conversation might stir you to dive into your story.

Repetitive writing also helps. It may sound mundane or more of a chore from one angle, but consistent actions create progress and develop habits. Foster a regular schedule even if it's 10 minutes a day for the first few days and work your way into something that is comfortable and suits you and your schedule.

MOTIVATED BUT NO IDEAS ON WHAT TO WRITE

It's as if you woke up one day and suddenly you find you're sucked dry of your creativity and you do not know what to write about. Just days before you could spout sonnets, lyrical masterpieces, toe curling ecstasy, blood drenched monster scenes or bend the minds of your readers to see the depths of the forests. And now, you're just blank and an abyss stares back at you with emptiness. You need a boost for your creative juice.

- First, rest. Spend a little time on yourself and don't beat yourself up. If you get frustrated with yourself, you'll actually make it worse. You need to take care of yourself so that you can refill your inkwell. Slow your thoughts by meditating. Imagine yourself in your thoughts. Look at them for what they are. The slow down will benefit you physically, mentally and ideally. Inspiration strikes where you find joy most.

- Do a few things for you. See friends and do other things you enjoy. Spend some time outdoors. Talk to a confidant about your situation. Ask a friend to help with an idea. Have conversations with people. Indulge in another hobby for a short time and maybe inspiration will strike. Walk through a museum or look at pictures of things you like.

- Put yourself in unfamiliar places and watch the world to help boost your creativity. It could be a new coffee shop, a quiet picnic table under a tree, a different spot at the library, in your car parked next to a scenic view. You can also spend some time daydreaming undisturbed by technology. It may not sound productive, but what if in your daydreams a story emerges from your abyss? If you're staying in, try a new scented candle. Or refresh your favorite space.

- Ask yourself the question: "Why am I not feeling creative?" Journal on that. When you find out why, you'll be able to look at your situation from a different perspective and come up with ways to challenge your feelings creatively.

- Try a prompt generator! Here's a few: servicescape.com, squibler.io, randomgenerator.com, thestoryshack.com or plot-generator.org.uk.

- Borrow from movie plots to birth an idea. (Think Sharknado).

- Try an interactive writing exercise. Asking others to help in your writing efforts can provide a fix to writer's block and provide some fun.

- Exercise. It's proven that physical exercise is not only good for the body but also for the mind and soul. It's the ultimate mood booster which can help your creative juices flow, sharpen your attention and motivate you to get things done. Carve some time out to get a little exertion in regularly and reap all the benefits of it. You don't need to exercise for long, extended periods of time or do exercises you don't like, unless you have certain goals you want to achieve that require them. But moving the body is the best shortcut to a happier spirit, and a rejuvenated mind.

LACKING SUPPORT

There may be times when you feel no one is supporting your writing endeavors. Perhaps you feel a little let down because your perception on the level of interest or care from those you confided in about your writing is not what you expected.

This is a tough pill to swallow and plays into your thoughts that say something bigger regarding what you believe of yourself.

It's important to remember the only support you require is yours! No one else can write your story for you. And if no one else has given you a glance of intrigue to write, it isn't something for you to worry about.

Write your story. It's important to prove it to yourself if you are struggling with external support for your writing. On a planet of billions of people, there's bound to be others out there who want to read it and will connect with it.

Once you're done writing your story and you put it out there, you'll find that you command new respect from others regarding your writing and your accomplishment. You'll see it from within too.

If support is what you're looking for and not external validation, and you haven't looked into the option already, there are a plethora of writing groups on a multitude of platforms that you can join and talk to other writers about your experiences in writing.

UNDER PRESSURE, FRUSTRATED AND STRESSED OUT ABOUT YOUR PROJECT

Something about the project you are currently working on has you feeling pressure, stressed out or frustrated and it's stopping you from continuing or finishing it. It's a hard place to be because you want to finish it but something about it has got you stuck.

Maybe it's not even the project but something else that's mucking about with your creative flow and has you holding in. Either way, you're left with this unsettled feeling and need to figure out what's got you here.

This is where your ability to be honest with yourself and journaling really comes in handy.

Take a step back, journal and answer some of these questions:

- How did this happen? How did I get so stressed about writing?
- Where did I forget to plan (if I plan)? Where did I go astray?
- What did I need? What do I need?
- What excuses did I make for myself?
- Did I wait until the last minute before a deadline and now I'm stressed out about completing my project on time?
- Did I write everything I thought of and found that it doesn't come to the word count that I need?
- Did I realize that there were areas that needed better expansion in my project?
- Are there big editing issues that I'm not willing to see currently?
- Is there anything I can do to rectify the situation now? If yes, what then? If not, why not?
- Is there something else outside my writing affecting it? If so, what is it?

Journal out your frustrations and stresses. If it comes out like you're having a conversation with yourself, asking questions and answering them, let it happen freely and openly.

It could be exactly what you need to move you through the frustration, or your stress, to reassess your project and figure out a way to continue it so that you are not frustrated or stressed out and instead regain the pleasantry of your craft. You'll also be able to recognize any similarities of the situation, if it occurs again, so that you can move beyond it faster and more beneficial to you. You'll become more aware of your perception of things, your habits and where you can grow more conscious of yourself.

Alternatively, when you're feeling stressed over your writing, reach out to a fellow writer and have a discussion about it. Ask to work on your projects simultaneously using a write/socialize/write strategy. Just remember, more writing than socializing. This way you keep each other moving forward and keep the pressure down.

Many people have a natural reaction to stress that tells them to steer clear of it. So, they stop entirely what they did that was causing them stress or they freeze and do nothing, hoping the moments will pass. This happens with writing too.

Sometimes you put a project down and take a break from it. Some writers never go back to some projects and they sit shelved because the writer chose not to deal with the emotions or thoughts that were causing them their discomfort.

There is a big difference between a little stress and overwhelming stress. It is important for you to decipher what's a little stress, which can be a good thing, and overwhelming stress, which can cause you to melt down. This is unique for everyone.

To figure this out, it's a good idea for you to sit with your journal, think and write about what it is you can tolerate when it comes to stress. It's important to determine this so you have a better understanding of what you can handle, where you can lean into that stress and use it as a motivator, when you need to take a break, what causes you to feel the need to take a break, what triggers you into a meltdown and finally where you need to place boundaries for yourself.

As for your breaks, exercise self-discipline. Know to prepare (mentally at least) and come back to your story. Think of how good it will feel to finish your manuscript.

If you feel you need more support with this, book a call with me via my website: www.tidepooloctopus.com

WRITE ALL DAY FOR WORK AND UNINSPIRED TO WRITE FOR YOURSELF WHEN YOU GET HOME

When you work all day, it's hard to get into your story because you've been sitting still, moving like crazy, or writing at the office all day. The zeal to write for yourself after work is lacking luster, and you're drained.

Some things to consider:

- Is there a chance that what you're writing at work is so closely similar to what you want to write at home?
- Is it that you're uninspired because you are sitting still for so long and you don't

want to do the same when you leave the office?

- Is it because you're moving around so much in your job your mind is wired-but-tired?
- Is it because your desire to write for yourself is not swaying you to put the time into yourself?

If something any of these landed for you:

- If you find that your mind is tired after your day of buzzing about, take time to meditate (a quiet meditation) and breathe for 10-15 minutes when you get home to help refresh your mind.

- If you can say honestly that your desire to write is strong and resonates from your gut, then why is it not so strong for you to do it for yourself? Are you waiting for someone else to tell you that you're worthy of your time? Are you waiting for someone to give you permission on how to use your time? I hope you answer "no" to both questions. But for any answer to those questions, write your honest answer to this question in your journal: Why do I write?

Go deeper on that: look up Dean Grasiozi's "Seven Levels Deep" Exercise. You can search for it and get the workings of it on any search engine. It is the easiest, most comprehensible breakdown of this exercise that is used in therapy practices, I've found to date. I strongly advise going through the exercise to make your reason(s) for writing more inspiring to you from within. It aims to make you more conscious of the subconscious reasons behind why you write (or do anything else). This is meant to compel you to continue with your craft.

For the record, I have no affiliation with Dean Grasiozi. But he offers some brilliant resources for people. It's because of his "discovery" of this exercise that has propelled it forward to the masses and he has made it easy to digest. I think it would be a disservice to you if I don't tell you about it.

- You can also change your space or the way you write (how you get the words down). Dictate to your phone or other voice recording device and use a transcription service. Write on topics that are not related to your work but are highly pleasurable. Instead of sitting, try a standing desk. The solutions are limitless, but it takes you to be willing to change to achieve your goals.

- If you find your block is simply that you're physically exhausted to write, try to journal for 5 minutes before bed. At least you're writing for those 5 minutes. Then rest!
  Rise 15 minutes earlier in the morning so that you can set yourself up to write for ten of those minutes and have some words down. But take care of your body. It's important to.

Rest is important and you should not cheat yourself of it. Remember to always be kind to yourself—physically as well as mentally.

Step back from your day and focus on your needs first. Refuel before you can produce anything.

OH, HEY! LOOK! A SQUIRREL!

You may have plenty of things to do and keep track of. Sometimes, your brain is all over the place and admittedly, you get distracted. Trying to get a good writing session in, is proving to be an enormous challenge for you, but you want to.

- Make a practice of regularly writing all your thoughts on pages so that you have it out of your head and now you can neatly place tasks to be handled neatly into your schedule.

- This is where some stress-busting exercise and meditation will come in handy to help calm your mind too. Try not to fuel your body with sugars and caffeine but with well-balanced meals and plenty of water and hopefully sooner than later that squirrel won't be so distracting.

- Make it a practice to not engage on social media during the time you set aside to write. Have the conversation with your family so that they know you need this time for you to do this. Most smartphones have a version of a "DO NOT DISTURB" function. It also has a way to set up calls to come through in emergencies and these are number specific. So, if it's the school calling about your kids, you can set up your phone so that their number rings through your "do not disturb" setting. If you don't have this option, monitor your phone and answer only the calls you absolutely have to.

- To limit distractions around you like a loud tv in the other room, headphones are a great option to pipe in instrumental music. Instrumental, so that lyrics don't pull at your train of thought.

YOUR PHYSICAL HEALTH KEEPS YOU FROM WRITING

Health issues can be very daunting and many of us have our own in varying severities. However, how consumed are you by your health? Bruce Lee had the stroke of bad luck when he broke his back. Strapped to a machine while it was healing, he still wrote a book. I'm not saying you should be like Bruce Lee, but even in his adversity he humbled, accepted help and did something incredible.

Your situation may look dire, but you have to ask yourself, is your desire to write stronger than your desire to obsess over your health? I'm not saying to neglect your health, I'm saying it's mind over matter.

- Acknowledging that you're ailing is a positive step forward. Being gentle with yourself, physically, emotionally and mentally is of utmost importance if you're ailing. Just as important is granting yourself grace and being patient with yourself and your situation.

- Creating a space in which you are comfortable to handle your situation and still write is ideal if you have a strong enough desire. It doesn't have to be leaps and bounds. Baby steps count as progress too. On good days, celebrate the good day and if you can, write your heart out and on not so good days, rest and take care of your human. Remember, you can also enlist help when you need to.

FORGETTING TO BUILD YOUR NEW WRITING HABIT

When you put the work in creating what you think will work for you, so that you can slide some time in to write and create a pattern, it can slip your mind. You may find you struggle with this new thing and keep forgetting.

This can be frustrating but don't give up. Forgive yourself. The new pattern you developed is not working as it currently stands and needs to be changed. Clearer goals need to be established and perhaps some real physical shifts.

- Try an alarm to tell you when it's time to write.

- Change the time that you want to sit and write to a time that it is easier to remember for you.

Just don't give up on yourself.

NO PLACE TO WRITE

We're full of excuses and this one is horse rubbish.

People write in their cars, on their lunch breaks in stairwells, in closets and storage rooms. They write on their smartphones walking around the block. People write in their beds with their knees propped up. People write while they're in the bathroom. Anywhere can be a place to write! If you want it bad enough, you'll make any space work. I'm writing this in a window-less storage room in my basement.

If you're looking for the perfect cozy corner in a room of your house that has a spectacular view from the window and you have the means to make it, then create it. If you don't have the means to make that happen, get creative and create a space that can work for you even if it's not your ideal space.

YOUR WRITING SPACE

Now, on another note about your writing space, declutter. Less clutter in your surroundings means fewer distractions during your process. Make it comfortable so that you want to spend time there. Think about physical surroundings, your being (physical, emotional, mental), sounds and scents, even tastes. How do you want your space to fit you? It doesn't have to be magazine perfect. You don't have to go out and spend a ton of money refitting your space. Simply, remove the excess clutter. Tidy things up so that you can write comfortably without the distraction. Take out the trash.

As for your being, how do you want to feel in your writing space? Like a boss? The comfortable sweater wearing writer you aspire to be? Like the soft textiles, curl up on a couch with a cup author? Or an author version of Dr. Frankenstein freewheeling his invention into existence? As often as possible, be in your element.

PATIENCE

Be patient, gentle and kind to yourself. Always. Patience is learned. The more forgiving you are to yourself, with your time, your effort and your level of skill, you will build patience.

- If you set targets which you're not meeting for over 1 or 2 days, reassess your goals and adjust them gently and honestly. Don't count yourself out and give up altogether.

- Look for support in a writer's group that suits you. There are plenty to choose from. Nanowrimo.org has a free community and there are also a ton of groups on Facebook to choose from. Even a friend/family member could offer support that you need for your writing.

DECISION MAKING, PERFECTION AND PROCRASTINATION—THE OVERTHINKER'S TRIO

This one is for the overthinkers.

This is hard, but it has to be done: decide and stick with it. Follow through. You'll know when you do (decide) if it's the right decision or not. If it's a good one, you learn from it. If it's not, you learn from it.

Either way, decide quickly and go with it. Slow decision making, the stalling and overthinking, will ultimately eat away at your most precious and valuable resource–time.

We all know time and tide wait for no one. Slow decision-making ties to perfectionism, overthinking and procrastination like a horse tied to a cart. It's why you stand with the fridge door open when you're feeling peckish and can't think of what it is you want (overthinking and indecision).

It's why you circle your office doing everything that is easy to do besides sitting down to work (procrastinating). It's why you shelve 8 projects and never let an audience glance at your words (perfectionism and not good enough). They are hand in hand in hand in hand.

Extend yourself some more grace and self-awareness in decision making. When you do, you'll notice if your brain wanders off in dreamland. That's an automatic response for some people, linked to fight, flight, freeze, fawn, because there's a fear of doing and/or it's your defense mechanism.

If you start overthinking and over-processing the information available to you, because you're trying to foresee all the possible outcomes of your situations, that's perfectionism at its finest.

3, 2, 1–Go! When you're trying to decide and you find yourself overthinking things, stop. Count back from 3 and take action. Make that decision.

If you're doing this with your story, go one way but make a note of the other thought somewhere to recall later in case you need it and move forward with your story.

Slow decision making, perfectionism, and procrastination are not reasons for you to beat yourself up. There are no reasons for you to beat yourself up, actually. It's a lesson in growth and self-development. Rise to the standard of not being hard on yourself for anything. Rise to the standard that perfection is in the flaws.

FEAR

Trying to tackle fear in a brief paragraph or two is absurd. Fear can run deep and sometimes make no sense on the surface. It is something that requires digging into, to find the root and acknowledging it as that before being able to devise a plan to deal with it.

There is no set of questions or instructions that can work as a one-size-fits-all to deal with fear because your fear will differ from someone else's. It is important to recognize that between human beings.

You can ask yourself what you are afraid of and remain vulnerable and open to your genuine answers. Then lead yourself through a personal conversation, with yourself, if you want to do this alone and not comfortable being vulnerable with someone else to guide you. Write your answers, and the questions that come up, so that you can analyze what you're seeing and what you're going through. Then maybe you can devise a plan of action to help yourself. Note this route is fraught with inaction and limited progress.

Honestly, fear is best discussed with someone so that you can gain a different perspective into what it is you're seeing and dealing with. And no, there is no cure for fear and fear is not always a bad thing; you just have to know how to use it to your advantage. And by all means, reach out.

CONCLUSION

It is ultimately you who moves yourself out of your writer's block. No one else can do that for you. It is a matter if you wish to shift your perception of things as you know them, as you know yourself, and go for something different from what you have known to be your safe zone.

Growth only happens in the uncomfortable and mental evolution is inevitable for the human mind and spirit. Find reverence and comfort in the mundane. Be thankful for what you have and look for adventure in the unknown.

Writers grow by writing. When you're not working on a story born of your wild imagination, work on the story of yourself via introspection and take notice as your words flow!

WHAT'S NEXT?

If you've identified your block and worked through it using the techniques suggested here, that's great and worthy of celebrating! I'm ecstatic about your progress. Please, leave a review and tell others what worked for you.

But if you still find, even after your shift, you need more guidance, where do you go?

I'm here to support writers, old, new and budding, giving you tools you need to help you shift your lens towards your creative process, timing and scheduling, being in a mental and physical state beneficial to you as well as your creative process where you get to grow as a writer and gain skills to help you beyond your writing.

I'm doing this through my new coaching program.

To learn more, book a free call with me via my website: www.tidepooloctopus.com.

ABOUT THE AUTHOR

Scharla Flynn is an editor and book coach who helps non-fiction writers and entrepreneurs simplify the writing process so they can confidently publish their first book. She currently lives in Ontario, Canada with her husband, two children and their dog and can often be found near a body of water and she loves to be warm.

You can connect with Scharla here:

https://www.instagram.com/tidepooloctopus
https://www.facebook.com/tidepooloctopus

www.ingramcontent.com/pod-product-compliance
Lightning Source LLC
La Vergne TN
LVHW010121170826
845678LV00012B/2536

* 9 7 8 1 7 3 8 9 8 3 6 2 9 *